Exotic Butterflies and Moths

Ruth Soffer

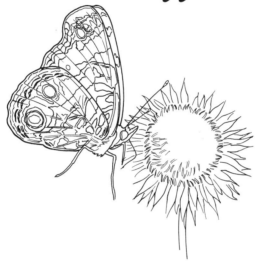

Dover Publications, Inc.
Mineola, New York

PUBLISHER'S NOTE

Everybody is in love with butterflies, and a few noble souls love moths just as much. The order of Lepidoptera contains more than 140,000 species—20,000 of them butterflies and the rest moths. For this coloring book, artist Ruth Soffer has chosen some of the most colorful and most interesting from around the world.

All are undeniably fascinating—not just for their vibrant appearance, which makes them such fun for a coloring book, but for their life histories and their biology. Butterflies and moths go through four life stages: egg, larva (or caterpillar), pupa, and adult. It is the caterpillar that does most of the eating. When butterflies and moths are in this stage, they may dine on a number of things, including cloth, wax, animal hair, or dead insects. But most feed on leaves—often the leaves of only a single plant species. When they are adults, most moths and butterflies like the nectar of flowers. But others prefer rotting fruit, excrement, or carrion. And still others don't eat at all as adults.

Besides eating, one of the most important things in a butterfly or moth's life is escaping from birds, bats, mice, lizards, and other predators. As you will see in this book, butterflies and moths have developed a number of different methods to protect themselves. Some are fast fliers. Some have such good hearing that they can evade bats at night. Many have developed camouflage that makes them seem indistinguishable from their surroundings. Some taste so bad that nobody wants to eat them. Others protect themselves with imitation eyes that startle away predators.

Unfortunately, the biggest danger to butterflies is humans, who poison them daily through the indiscriminant use of insecticides and who also destroy much of their habitat.

The taxonomy (classification of names) of moths and butterflies keeps changing, and you will often find different scientific names for the same animals. Where possible, we have tried to follow the names given in *The National Audubon Society Field Guide to North American Butterflies* (fifteenth printing; New York: Knopf, 2000). For butterflies from other continents, you may want to check the names here against those given by other authoritative sources.

Bibliographical Note

Exotic Butterflies and Moths is a new work, first published by Dover Publications, Inc., in 2002.

DOVER *Pictorial Archive* SERIES

This book belongs to the Dover Pictorial Archive Series. You may use the designs and illustrations for graphics and crafts applications, free and without special permission, provided that you include no more than four in the same publication or project. (For permission for additional use, please write to Permissions Department, Dover Publications, Inc., 31 East 2nd Street, Mineola, N.Y. 11501.)

However, republication or reproduction of any illustration by any other graphic service, whether it be in a book or in any other design resource, is strictly prohibited.

International Standard Book Number: 0-486-42381-6

Manufactured in the United States of America
Dover Publications, Inc., 31 East 2nd Street, Mineola, N.Y. 11501

The *Agrias sardanapalus*, found in the upper Amazon basin of South America, has the beauty of a miniature stained-glass window. Looking down on it from above, you see wings bordered in charcoal black; the fore wings gleam with a gorgeous red, with a blue spot near the midwing, and the hind wings with royal blue. The wings' under-sides (seen here in the butterfly at top) are decorated with protective eyespots. *Agrias sardanapalus* is a favorite of collectors—much sought after for its beauty but rare and very difficult to catch. The flower shown at the bottom of the picture is the mirabilis.

The *western tiger swallowtail* (*Pterourus rutulus* or *Papilio rutulus*), probably the most conspicuous butterfly of the western U.S., has pale yellow wings with black tiger-stripes and yellow-spotted black borders. You can find it anywhere from British Columbia down to Baja California, especially in moist areas such as parks, gardens, canyons, and creek sides. (In moist canyons you can sometimes see huge gatherings of swallowtails.) It is rare east of the Rocky Mountains, but can be found as far east as the Black Hills of South Dakota. The caterpillars live on willow, poplar, aspen, alder, and sycamore. Adults are attracted to butterfly bush (*Buddleia davidii*, which also is known as summer lilac), pentas, thistles, and rhododendron.

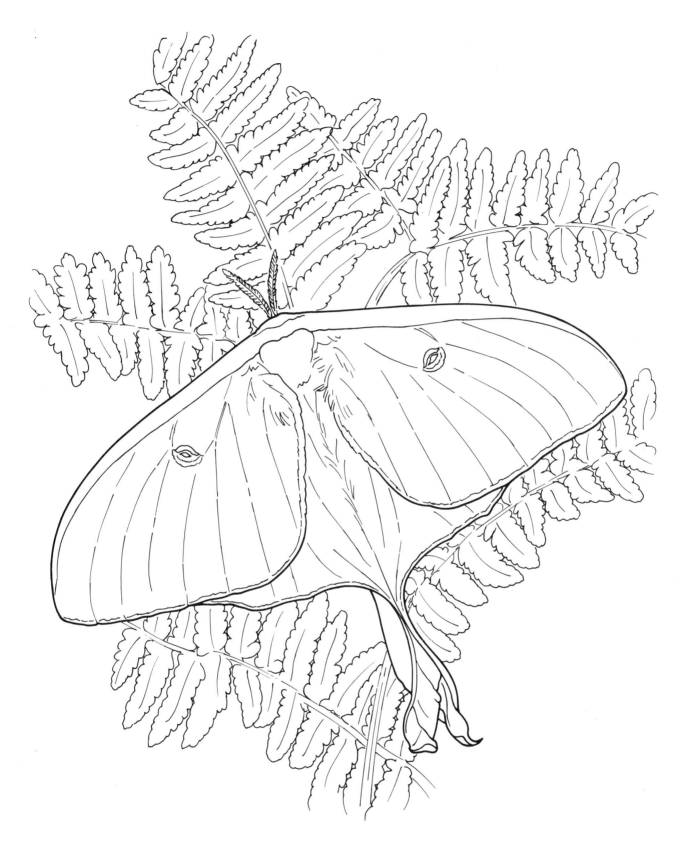

Moths differ from butterflies in being generally duller in color and having feathered antennae (not clubbed like those of butterflies). The *luna moth* (*Actias luna*) is one of the most spectacular moths—pale, ghostly looking, and big, with a wingspan of about 4 inches. Its wings are pale green; the fore wings are decorated with eyespots and purple front edges, and the hind wings have lovely long tails. This moth lives only in North America; you can see it in the deciduous forests in the eastern half of the U.S. and Canada, where its caterpillar eats the leaves of hickory, walnut, sweet gum, persimmon, birch, and other trees.

The *monarch* (*Danaus plexippus*) is the only butterfly that makes long migrations north and
south as birds do. Individual butterflies don't
make the round trip, though: Those that fly north
in the spring stop along the way to breed, and
then they die, leaving it up to their offspring to
make the return journey. Monarchs live throughout most of North and South America and have
been established in Hawaii and Australia. In
North America, the western monarchs spend the
winters in evergreen groves on the central
California coast; huge swarms from the East or
Midwest fly down to fir forests high in the mountains of central Mexico. The monarch lays its eggs
on milkweed or dogbane. Because the caterpillar
eats these poisonous plants, the adult monarch
tastes bad to birds, and they have learned to
avoid it.

The **Polyphemus moth** (*Antheraea polyphemus*) has borrowed its name from the one-eyed giant of Greek mythology. Can you see the eyespots on its wings? The wings are fairly large (with a wingspan of $3\frac{1}{2}$–$5\frac{1}{2}$ inches) and are brownish yellow. The fore wings have small eyespots bordered in yellow. On the hind wings the eyespots are larger, and the yellow borders are surrounded by black and blue. This moth lives east of the Rocky Mountains from Canada to Mexico, in deciduous forests where the caterpillar feeds on the leaves of alder, basswood, birch, chestnut, elm, hickory, maple, poplar, and sycamore. The adults often flock to artificial lights at night.

The *pearl crescent* (*Phyciodes tharos*) or *pearly crescentspot* is named for the cream-colored spots on its orange-and-black wings. It is one of the most common North American butterflies. From northern Canada to southern Mexico, and from eastern Washington and southeast California to the Atlantic, you will see it in meadows and other open spaces—usually flying low over the grass, alternately flapping its wings and gliding. It is small (wingspan 1.3–1.5 inches) but pugnacious, often darting after other butterflies that venture near its perch and driving them away. It lays its eggs on the leaves of asters. Its caterpillars eat the aster leaves, and adult pearl crescents take nectar from asters, fleabanes, thistles, and other composites. At the bottom of the picture a male is shown among the asters, and at the top are two females.

Like the Polyphemus moth, the *Io moth* (*Automeris io*) is named after a character from Greek mythology—Io, a beautiful young maiden who was turned into a cow. When threatened, these moths open their wings to show off two large, cowlike eyespots, which scare away birds and other predators. Io moths are found in open woods, meadows, and cornfields east of the Rocky Mountains from Canada to Mexico. Their caterpillars eat the leaves of many plants, especially wild cherry, and are known for their poisonous spines, which can be as painful as a bee sting. The moth at top right is a male; the other two are females. Females are larger than males, and their fore wings are purplish brown whereas the males' are yellow. Other than the black eyespots, the rear wings of both are yellow with red-orange shading.

Here you see two beautiful representatives of the East African genus Acraea. Both have black-bordered, pale-orange wings, but the lower butterfly, *Acraea quirina*, seems especially ethereal because its wings are partly transparent. The butterfly at top is *Acraea caecilia*. Butterflies of the Acraea genus are slow, lazy flyers and—because their caterpillars feed on toxic plants of the passionflower family—unpalatable to birds. (The spectacular, flamelike flower they are visiting here is the gloriosa lily.)

The *bronze copper* (*Hyllolycaena hyllus* or *Lycaena hyllus*) is a small butterfly (wingspan about 1.4 inches) found near open, wet meadows, marshes, streams, and ponds from Maine to Maryland and west across southern Canada and the northern U.S. to Colorado, Montana, and the Northwest Territories. Caterpillars live on grasses of the buckwheat family—especially curly dock. Often you will see adult males perching on low growth near these plants and looking for females. (The males are purplish orange in color, whereas the females are yellow-orange.) The adults visit flowers only infrequently, but sometimes take nectar from blackberry flowers and red clover. (The plant in the background of the picture is pokeweed.)

The **sheep moth** (*Hemileuca eglanterina*) lives in mountain meadows and sheep pastures west of the Rocky Mountains from southern California to southern Canada. Adults can be seen in the daytime flying quickly and close to the ground. Their wingspan is about 2.5 inches. Front wings are usually pinkish gray and the hind wings yellow—both decorated with black stripes and spots. The females lay eggs in masses. The caterpillars eat leaves of various plants, especially those of the rose family. Caterpillars pupate in late summer, and moths emerge the next summer.

The *blue morpho* (*Morpho menelaus*) is a large (6-inch wingspan), stunning, iridescent blue butterfly from the rainforests of South and Central America—especially Costa Rica, Venezuela, and Brazil. It lives in the emergent layer, at the tops of the tallest rainforest trees, and drinks the juices of rotting fruit. The females are not as brilliantly colored as the males. When blue morphos of either sex are at rest, you only see their wings' camouflaged undersides—leaf brown with bronze-colored eyespots. The caterpillars are reddish brown with bright patches of lime-green on their backs. They spin a communal web, where, after nine to eleven weeks, they pupate together.

The ***painted lady*** (*Vanessa cardui*) is also known as the ***thistle butterfly*** and the ***cosmopolite***. It may be the most widespread butterfly in the world—found in North America, Europe, Africa, and Asia. The painted lady lays her eggs on thistle, mallow, or hollyhock; the caterpillar dines on the leaves, and adults take nectar from thistle and clover flowers. The adults' wings are mostly black, brown, and orange on top, with some white spots; the wings' undersides are gray with white and red markings. Like the monarchs, painted ladies are long-haul migrants. In the early spring, they begin to fan out from the southwestern U.S. across the continent and up to the sub-Arctic, and from North Africa and southern Europe northward. But they do not come back again in the fall, and only those who stayed home in the south seem to survive the winter.

The *malachite* (*Siproeta stelenes*) is one of the most spectacular North American butterflies—but only for a few days. When it first emerges from its chrysalis the tops of its wings are a brilliant marbled green with wide brown-black margins (the undersides are tawny brown with pale green patches), but the green fades with a few days' exposure to sunlight. The female is paler than the male. Malachites live in forest edges and woodland glades from northern South America to as far north as Texas and southern Florida. Caterpillars live on green shrimp plant (yerba papagayo) and ruellia; adults like the juices of rotting fruit, but occasionally will sip nectar from flowers such as the bleeding hearts shown here.

These *Cairns birdwings* (*Ornithoptera priamus*) are rare butterflies found only in southeast Asia and Australia—mostly in rainforest clearings. Cairns birdwings are the largest Australian butterflies, with wingspans up to 6 inches for males and 8 inches for females. The males are green, gold, and black; the females are black, white, and yellow. (Here two males are shown at the right, and at the bottom left is a female.) The newly hatched caterpillar eats the shell of its own egg and then feeds on the large rainforest vine (*Aristolochia*) on which the egg was laid. The adults feed on nectar from flowering rainforest plants.

16

The *white admiral* (*Basilarchia arthemis*) is found in deciduous forest borders and glades in Alaska and British Columbia in the west, and in the east from Maine and New York to Manitoba and Minnesota. Its wings are jet black with a bluish iridescence, and with a white band across the middle. Varieties found further south have different coloring and are often called red-spotted purples or banded purples. The caterpillars feed on birch, willow, and poplar, and hawthorn. Before the winter, the caterpillars bundle themselves up in rolled-up, silk-tied leaves, and in spring they come out again. The adults sip nectar from flowers but also are attracted to carrion. When flying, they have some of the habits of the pearl crescent: They alternately glide and flap their wings, and they dart out to drive away other insects that come into their territories.

When *buckeyes* (*Junonia coenia* or *Precis lavinia*) are not busy chasing other flying insects away from their territory, you can often see males perching on low plants or bare ground, keeping an eye out for females. The buckeye is medium-sized (wingspan 1.6–2.7 inches) and mostly brown, with six large purple-black eyespots—two on each hind wing and one on each fore wing. It gets nectar from lantana (shown here), zinnias, asters, verbenas, and other composite flowers. The caterpillars feed on plantains, toadflax, snapdragons, figwort, vervain, and acanthus. Buckeyes range from southern Mexico up to central California and North Carolina, but in the late spring the adults migrate throughout the U.S. and up into southern Canada. Along the east coast in the fall, the southward migration of clouds of buckeyes is as spectacular as that of the monarchs.

The ***banded peacock***, or ***Fatima*** (*Anartia fatima*), is a medium-sized butterfly (2.5-inch wingspan), mostly brown, with white or cream-colored bands on its wings. It lives in subtropical open areas such as sunny, flowering fields, orchards, and watercourses from Panama north to Mexico, and occasionally as far north as South Texas. The caterpillars live on ruellia and other Acanthaceae, and the adults visit flowers for their nectar. The banded peacock here is pirouetting among lupines and other wildflowers.

Underwing moths (*Catocala species*) are members of the Noctuidae, the owlet moth family—the largest family of moths, containing about 3,000 species in North America and many more in Europe and Asia. The underwing moth is notable for its grayish mottled fore wings, which fold over the body and make the moth invisible when at rest on a tree trunk. But when it is disturbed it startles would-be predators by flashing its bright-ly colored hind wings. Like all the other Noctuidae, the underwing moth has hearing organs on each side of its thorax. Its hearing is attuned to high frequencies, so it can evade bats when flying at night. Underwing caterpillars feed on a wide range of leaves and grasses. Adults may feed on fermenting tree sap or decaying fruit, sip flower nectar, or take no sustenance at all.

Tiger moths (*Apantesis species* or *Grammia species*) can be found in fields and roadsides from Canada through most of the U.S., as well as in Europe, Asia, and Australia. Small moths, with wingspans of about 1.5–3 inches, they generally have black fore wings crosshatched with ivory white and hind wings yellow to red and spotted with black. Like the underwing moths, they are night flyers and have a well-developed sense of hearing. Males are attracted to artificial lights at night, but females generally remain close to breeding areas and food plants. Adults feed on nectar. The caterpillars, which are mostly black with a yellow midline stripe, feed on lettuce, clover, and other leaves.

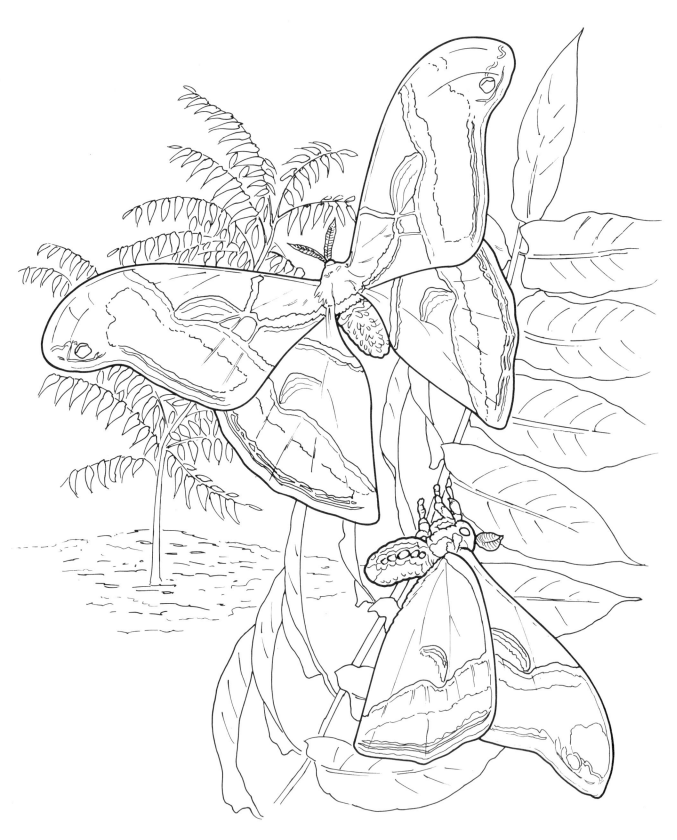

The *Cynthia moth* (*Samia cynthia*) is a large (wingspan 4–5 inches) silkworm moth with gorgeous olive-green and purple wings. The Cynthia originally lived in China, but Americans brought specimens to Philadelphia in the 1860s with the hopes of starting a new silk trade. The silk trade idea was abandoned, but the Cynthia moth spread widely throughout the northeastern U.S. In the background of the picture you can see an ailanthus tree. Like the moth, this tree originated in Asia. It was introduced to the U.S. in 1784 and spread like a weed. Sometimes known as "tree of heaven" and sometimes as "stinking sumac," the ailanthus is a fast-growing tree that thrives in cities and vacant lots. It provides a home for the Cynthia moth, whose caterpillars eat its leaves.

The *little metalmark* (*Calephelis virginiensis*) is a small butterfly (.7–.8 inches) that is noticeable, like other members of the metalmark family, because of the glistening, silvery spots on its otherwise rust- to orange-colored wings. It is found in marshy meadows, sunny open fields, and the edges of woods from Maryland to Florida and west to Arkansas and Texas. The caterpillar often lives on the yellow thistle, and the adults sip nectar from flowers. (The flower pictured here is the trumpet honeysuckle.)

When *Milbert's tortoiseshell* (*Nymphalis milberti*) is sitting with its wings folded, it is brown and looks like a dead leaf. But when it spreads its wings, their tops show a colorful band of yellow blending into bright orange, with blue dots along the wing edges. This butterfly lays its eggs on nettles—often several hundred eggs at a time. The caterpillars, which first live in colonies in silken nests, feed on the nettles. Adults get their refreshment from sap, rotting fruit, and the nectar of thistles, goldenrods, and lilacs. Milbert's tortoiseshell likes cool areas, and you may see it along dry stream beds, riversides, beaches, trails, and mountain rockslides from northern Canada south to southern California, Oklahoma, and West Virginia. In temperate regions you may sometimes even see it venturing out on warm days in the middle of winter.

Hairstreaks belong to a subfamily of butterflies named for the hairlike tails they usually sport at the base of their hind wings. The ***juniper hairstreak*** (*Mitoura siva* or *Callophrys gryneus*) is a small (wingspan .8–1.2 inches) one that lives in scrubby woodlands, rockslides, canyons, and arid areas of the western U.S. from southeastern Washington to southern California and east to western Texas, Nebraska, and southern Saskatchewan. It lays its eggs on juniper trees and as an adult sips nectar from composites growing near junipers. The male is grayish brown above, with rust-colored spots near the back of the hind wing, and the female is rust-brown except for the borders of her wings. The undersides of the wings have a brownish-green sheen, highlighted with a white, black-bordered line.

The *blue pansy* (*Precis orithya* or *Junonia orithya*) is a small, showy butterfly with black fore wings, bordered with white, and reflective blue hind wings. (The female, with her brown hind wings, is less colorful.) It is found in open spaces and grassy roadsides from sub-Saharan Africa across southern Asia to Japan, Malaysia, and Australia. Its host plant is usually one of the acanthus or figwort species. (The plant in the picture is a rambler rose.)

Glasswings or **clearwings** (*Oleria species*) are some of the most intriguing butterflies of the Central and South American rainforest. Their wings are as transparent as the wings of fairies, making it difficult to tell one species from another. The wings of the clearwing at bottom are rimmed with yellow-orange; the see-through panes look pale blue because they reflect the sky. *Oleria quadrata* (at top right) also has pale-orange bands around her wings' transparent panes, but the wings are rimmed with brownish black. The female clearwing follows birds to feed on their droppings, which give her the nitrogen she needs to produce eggs. The males, meanwhile, visit flowers in the composite family, from which they extract alkaloids; these alkaloids will give their offspring a bad taste to protect them against predators.

The *zebra longwing* (*Heliconius charitonius*) has narrow wings with a span of about 3 inches. The wings are coal black above, striped and spotted with pale yellow. It lives in the tropics from northern South America to as far north as Texas and South Carolina. (In Florida it has been designated the state butterfly.) Every night, multitudes of zebra longwings come together at communal resting spots on bushes. As is true of other members of the Heliconiinae subfamily, the caterpillars feed on passionflower vines. The adults—who are protected from most predators because they taste bad—sip nectar from Spanish needle, red salvia, blue porterweed, golden dewdrop, and firebrush. The zebra longwing in the foreground above is taking nectar from a Mexican flame vine; in the background is a Mexican heather plant.

The *red lacewing* (*Cethosia chrysippe*), also a member of the Heliconiinae, is said to be the most beautiful butterfly of its region—Australia, New Guinea, and the Solomon Islands. It is orange and dark brown, but in the sunlight it takes on a pink and purple glow. Like the other members of its subfamily, the caterpillar lives on passionflower vines, and the adult is unpalatable to most predators—which enables it to be less flitty and nervous than most other butterfly species. The flower pictured above is a plumeria, found in Australia and nearby islands.

The upper butterfly here is a *Heliconius burneyi*, a beautiful Brazilian cousin of the zebra longwing who also lives on passionflower vines and tastes bad to predators. Its wings are mostly brownish black, but the fore wings are a bright yellow-orange close to the body and have pale-yellow splotches further out; the stripes on the hind wings are orange. At the bottom is a *Cartea vitula*, also from South America. This butterfly, a member of the Riodinidae family, has wings bordered with black and decorated with bright orange panes. (The outer pane on each fore wing is yellow.)

30

The **zephyr anglewing** (*Polygonia zephyrus*) is a fairly small butterfly (wingspan about 2 inches) whose wings are mostly orange on top, lightening to yellow towards the edges. When it is at rest only the wings' dark undersides show, making it look like a dead oak leaf. But it is a nervous flyer, and doesn't sit still very long. It darts here and there, visiting thistles and composite flowers in meadows, streamsides, and open woods in the mountains. Its caterpillar lives on currants, elms, and rhododendrons. The zephyr anglewing is found mostly west of the Rockies, from British Columbia and Manitoba down to southern California and New Mexico.

Alphabetical List of Scientific Names

Alphabetical List of Common Names